D1458692

Garstang & Over-Wyre
in Times Past

Catherine Rothwell

Dedicated to
Frank Walmsley
Known to his Many Friends as
MR. GARSTANG

a30118 037301631b

£1·00

479522605

Published by Countryside Publications, School Lane, Brinscall, Chorley, Lancashire

Printed by Tamley-Reed Limited

Text © Catherine Rothwell, 1979

ISBN 0 86157 017 0

Introduction

Much of the information on Garstang in the ensuing pages has been culled from Frank Walmsley's unpublished history at the request of his widow. I consider it an honour to have been asked to choose items from this account and to use them with photographs most of which Frank collected over a long period of time. His title, *From Cherestanc to Gahstin,* well conveys his aim: pity it is that Frank's history cannot be published in full. Perhaps a Local Historical Society can do this one day? Not only is it a valuable record from one who knew Garstang over a period of seventy years, but from its pages shines a love for both town and townspeople which gives to the account a special quality that it could never otherwise have had. Frank's twinkling humour viewed with appreciation and a kindly eye such local characters as Jem Stuart, landlord of the old Horns Inn. Only deep, personal knowledge of Garstang families and traditions, like "Wissenda", could bring out their full flavour.

"Whit Monday was a day of glad re-unions between people who had left, and their friends and relatives who clung to their hometown. Exiles from Garstang made it a custom to return to the place of their birth. What a heart-warming occasion. What a turmoil of kissing, hand-shaking, hugging and back-slapping there was in the main street that morning. What an excited gabble of conversation."

Such an atmosphere invokes the abiding contentment of dwellers in the country and seems linked down the centuries with the township of Garstang in 1226 when it belonged to the Baron of Kendal and Wyresdale, and the inhabitants were bound to each other by Frank Pledge for the maintenance of law and order; when the constables "apprehended all vagabonds and sturdy fellows, kept the stocks and the ducking stool in repair and pursued the hue and cry", aided by the populace.

Garstang, the largest parish in Amounderness apart from Kirkham, included Pilling, so there is a place for Over-Wyre in this little book and I think Frank would have approved for he was very interested in the Garstang and Knott End Railway and in canal transport.

Before the Conquest, part of the Saxon manor of Cheristang even included Lytham, thus the sheer historical range, not to mention the diverse, scenic beauty, is beyond the scope of any small book. It is tantalising to cut out incidents clamouring for attention. Within its boundaries lay Thomas Tyldesley's fox-hunting country, Pilling Moss "boundless as God's Grace", Cockersand Abbey, Greenhalgh Castle, a spa with medicinal properties, an

3

ancient tithe barn and the Turner Farm House occupied for 300, possibly 500, years by members of the same family who belonged to a group of farmers known as "the Barnacre Lords", each with his own pew in the Church of St. Helen. Over generations they brought the land under cultivation. The Duke of Hamilton, disputing their rights, learned that verdict had gone in favour of the "Lords", but on the way home, merrymaking at Gaugut (Galgate), the Deeds disappeared. Contesting again, verdict went in favour of the Duke.

Characters included Old Tommy Clarke (son of Robert, the attorney) who lived in a shop opposite the Royal Oak. Tommy had a newspaper business and a lending library. He took an active part in Garstang life, becoming mayor, and for a time he was editor of the *Preston Pilot*, trudging from Garstang to Preston and back with his bundles. In those days one man did many jobs. The Garstang Rural Council's first meeting on January 3rd 1895 at the King's Arms Hotel was called by John Noble, first Clerk. He was also Clerk to the Assessment Committee, School Attendance Committee, Agent for the Royal Insurance Company, Secretary of Garstang Gas Company, as well as partner in a local firm of coal merchants, Noble and Alston.

The lower part of the Town Hall served as Corn Exchange, where thousands of windles were bought and sold. Dances, concerts and plays went on upstairs and a tiny dark room did duty as "lock up". What a calamity when it was burned down, not once but twice.

The heyday of the stage and mail coaches passing along the main route north brought prosperity to town, as did canal trade, but even when these diminished, the bustle of markets carried on. Cattle Fairs, Horse Fairs, Agricultural Shows saw the Royal Oak Field full of marquees. Worldfamous champion horses including James Agate's *Ego* were shown in the ring and mettlesome horses put through their paces in the main street, scattering crowds. Three thousand head of cattle moved down High Street in 1805, driven from Scotland and Ireland. Doors and windows had to be barricaded against their press. In the seventeenth century "Drunken Barnabee" was caught up literally. He enshrined his adventure in verse. There were at that time thirteen public houses. Sir Walter Scott, whilst in Garstang, lost two breastpins, one of pure Irish gold, "the gift of the ladies of Llangollen". Even Bonnie Prince Charlie stayed for a short time in 1715.

It is small wonder that Frank sustained interest in his native Garstang all life long, and, in so doing, left memories for us to treasure of "times past".

I most sincerely thank all those who have lent photographs or allowed copies for publication: Miss Cartmell; Mr R. Gibson; Mrs J. Hesketh; Lancaster City Museum; Lancashire Evening Post; Lancashire Record Office; Mrs C. Storey; Mrs D. Walker; Mrs F. Walmsley.

Catherine Rothwell, 1979.

The name Hackensall Hall possibly derives from Haakon, a Scandinavian chief who settled on the strategically positioned spur, Knott End. Geoffrey the Crossbowman was awarded the estate in the time of King John and the property passed down until the fifteenth century when a daughter inherited, who in turn divided it amongst her own four daughters. After Rossall Grange was ravaged by the sea, Richard and Anne Fleetwood rebuilt Hackensall Hall and came to live there. Now, in a low gable on the south side, a commemoration stone bearing the inscription "F.R.A. God's Providence, 1656" was incorporated in the building.

In 1797 it became the property of James Bourne of Stalmine. The Hackensall Hoard, a valuable collection of Roman coins, was discovered when the Hall was a farm. There have been rumours since of other unreported finds. This large, irregular building, with mullioned and transomed windows, retains few of its original architectural features, having undergone thorough restoration in 1873. Two skeletons, thought to be lovers, deliberately walled-up and left to die, came to light when alterations were in progress. They are the ghosts of the Hall, which also is reported to have a visiting boggart in the shape of a horse which performed useful tasks provided a roaring fire was left to recline in front of. No welcoming fire resulted in blood-curdling bellows of anger.

Focal point for centuries and standing in the middle of the Market Place is the Cross. Nearby were the stocks where wrong-doers were placed to sit out the allotted hours thought necessary to expiate their crime. The fish stones, curved in shape, also stood here and were used to lay out fish and other foods for sale until one November 5th (known as "mischief night") damaged them so badly they fell apart and had to be moved. A well and a pump, crushed by a cart in the square, also had to go.

On the worn steps of the Market Cross men and women have preached the gospel, orators have harangued passers-by, young men have been urged to "join up" and fight for their country.

The Town Clerk of Garstang in 1715 was Roger Muncaster who boldly spoke out from these steps in defence of Prince Charles Edward whose forces were then marching to Preston. Six young, local men joined him to assist the rebel army, but four came to grief. Muncaster was convicted and hanged at Gallows Hill, Preston. John Leybourne of Nateby, Joseph Wadsworth of Catterall, Thomas Cartmell of Billsborrow and Thomas Goose Junior of Catterall were found guilty and hanged at Stocks Lane End, Catterall on February 14th 1716. Edward Sykes of Nether Wyresdale and Thomas Walmsley, strangely enough, were acquitted.

Land in Bonds Lane was obtained by Garstang's Catholic community in 1857, sufficient to build a new church, school and house for the priest. The black and white habits of the Sisters of Charity of St. Paul who taught the scholars were once a familiar sight in Garstang.

Richard Walker, Tom Swarbrick, William Towers (front row) and Tom Rawlinson, John Swarbrick and Robert Dewhurst (back row), members of the United Order of Catholic Brethren, are seen on the photograph above, which probably dates from 1910.

When the new church of Saints Mary and Michael was completed, the old church was turned into a Reading Room known as the Institute. In May 1882 the local Liberal Party hired the hall for a political meeting, but this so angered Mr Albert Simpson (right) of *Elmhurst*, a staunch Conservative, that he and his supporters barricaded the doors, quoted the rule that the hall could not be hired for political purposes and launched an acrimonious correspondence in the *Lancaster Guardian* airing large words and fiery sentiments for most of the summer. The building of the Liberal Club in Bridge Street (opened October 25th 1887) was quoted as "marking the end of political darkness and political death in Garstang".

GARSTANG PARADE

Above: 1910 Garstang Parade featuring Louis Bleriot and his "Flying Machine".

Right: Parades and festivals gathered on the Royal Oak Field, principal playground of the town and for many years home of the Garstang Football Club. Some of these young men now lie under the grass on which they played, for St. Thomas's Parochial Church Council bought a large part of the football pitch to extend the graveyard.

At the north end of Garstang stands the former Grammar School, now used as an Arts Centre and managed by the Town Trust. The old stone wall to be seen in the photograph above encloses what once was the scholars' playground. Erected in 1756, it is one of the few buildings of any antiquity to remain. The Lord of the Manor, Sir Edward Walpole, presented the land on which the school was built. By 1851 it was in a dilapidated condition, reported as being "dirty and slovenly with a few dingy maps . . . a wicked-looking old comb hangs by a piece of string near the door . . . books thrown here and there as though somebody has been having a fight". The annual salary of the first headmaster, Mr. Fawcett, was £3-7-0. Of the headmasters, Mr. Joseph Irwin, who came in 1898, stayed a long time and became well known as a good teacher and strict disciplinarian. The Grammar School closed its doors when Mr Irwin retired in 1928, but was re-opened by Lancashire County Council as a Domestic and Woodwork Centre in 1929. Artists now hold exhibitions of their work in this building.

Right: The lower third form of the Grammar School is shown in the upper photograph, taken in May 1915. The village school of Nateby, in an even earlier photograph from this century, was run by a brother and sister.

12

13

Top left: The King's Arms Hotel, fully licensed premises in High Street, was occupied by Mr J. H. Bargh in 1919 and the Bill of Sale drawn up at that time reveals kitchen, scullery, clubroom, sitting room, four bedrooms and three sitting rooms on the ground floor. A large yard with stabling was necessary to deal with the coaches that arrived. There was even a pinfold attached to the premises for housing stray animals.

Bottom left: June 28th 1911 saw the American millionaire Prescott Bigston and party changing horses at the Eagle and Child. Above: The covered landau, driven by Chris Richardson in 1909, served as the hotel's taxi. Amongst the original 13 inns were The Blue Anchor, Golden Ball, Red Lion, Holy Lamb, Swan, Brown Cow, Pack Horse and Shovel and Broom. The Old Horns Inn sign was unique, consisting of a huge pair of horns dug up from the Bog of Allen, Ireland. The landlord was said to have refused an offer of 100 guineas for them. The principal posting house of the town was the Royal Oak Hotel, many famous people having stayed, including Sir Walter Scott, William Black, and Celia Fiennes.

Left: The Corn Mill, operated for many years by the Richardson family. Now a private residence, much restored, its stone walls seem perfect in a rural environment. The clatter of its machinery and the roar of its mill race are silent. Massive draught-horses yoked to drays used to stand patiently awaiting the signal to move off with their heavy loads to far-flung farm houses. The local boys loved a thrill-packed ride on the hoist running between basement and third floor. As the water wheel turned, the whole building seemed to tremble. A sliding panel gave sight of the dark, boiling fury of the mill race.

Above: One of Frank Walmsley's most vivid memories was riding on top of a fully-loaded dray, off for the day with a cold meat and potato pie swathed in a red-spotted handkerchief. Nora and Connie Harrison, with Ethel Walmsley, wave from the gate of Grandma Walmsley's cottage in Church Street.

Above: Candles and paraffin lighting were gradually replaced by gas from 1880 when the Garstang Gas Company's new plant in Moss Lane began to operate. The need of a larger works became apparent as the consumption of gas increased, and in 1910 the works was remodelled. The photograph shows Gasworks Bridge.

Right: The photographs of 1905 show that Claughton and Calder Vale Post Offices were also picturesque village stores. John Dodding was both grocer and draper.

Top left: Meadows spreading from the River Wyre where sleek cattle browse on the lush pastures are particularly rich as springtime gives place to summer. The heights of Wyresdale and Bleasdale beckon mysteriously through a haze of amethyst, but the river in full spate in winter presents a different picture, with branches, shrubs and sods torn from its banks, rushing down from the hills in Marshaw and Tarnbrook.

Bottom left: For generations the great stone weir held back the flow of water to divert it through the mill-sluice, but in 1961 it was breached after decades of battering by floodwater and finally collapsed, allowing the river to revert to its natural level. Both views date from 1905. One such flood occurred on the morning of Monday December 16th 1936. Following weeks of incessant rain the river rose swiftly and alarmingly, overflowing its banks and inundating adjacent houses and buildings. Bridge Street was soon a foot deep from the bottom of Ball Brow to the bridge. Turgid, brown floodwater covered fields and the Lancaster–Preston Canal burst its banks near Nateby Hall.

Above: The cool placidity of Brock Bottoms is shown at the height of summer, 1923.

The name Garstang may have sprung from a Saxon word meaning common-land or meadow-land (Gaerstung). Domesday Book describes it as Cherestanc, occupying six carucates of land. One carucate was equal to six oxgangs or bovates, the latter denoting the amount of land that one man with one ox could plough in a season. This amount varied from district to district according to the nature of the soil. The earliest mention of a Lord of the Manor of Garstang was in 1226 when William de Lancastre gave four bovates of land in the Vill de Gayrestange to the Abbot of Cockersand "to hold as of their Church of St. Helen". About the same time he gave to Robert le Botiller "the mill of Gayrestange with its site and pool".

Churchtown, pictured here, used to have markets and pot fairs. A century ago it was "a clean tidy village, hidden amid trees, sweetly isolated, and as quiet all day through . . . as if people had either left it or locked themselves up in their houses". Not far away is the ancient Church of St. Helen, Garstang Parish Church, "the Cathedral of the Fylde". Pillars in the nave date from 1200 A.D.; the tower, c. 1450, contains six bells. Registers date from 1567, Chalices 1659 and 1690. In the Churchyard is a sundial of 1757 and the base of an ancient cross. Tradition says a boulder in a field not far from the Church used to turn round whenever the bells rang.

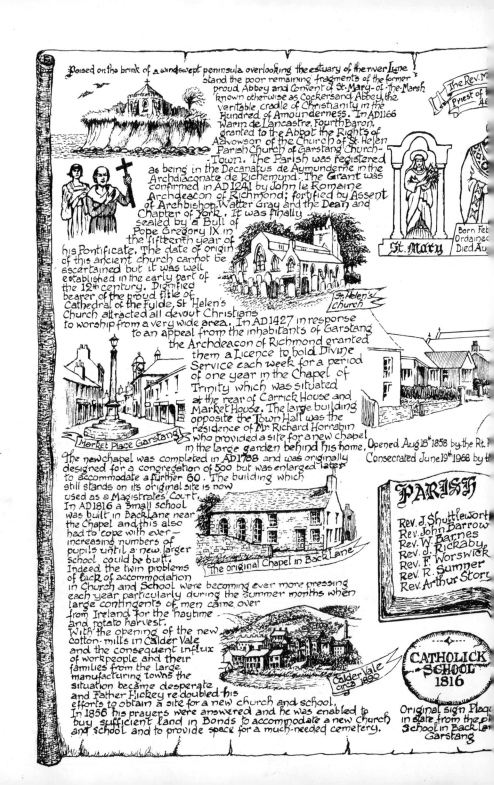

Poised on the brink of a windswept peninsula overlooking the estuary of the river Lune stand the poor remaining fragments of the former proud Abbey and Convent of St. Mary-of-the-Marsh known otherwise as Cockersand Abbey, the veritable cradle of Christianity in the Hundred of Amounderness. In AD 1166 Warin de Lancastre, Fourth Baron, granted to the Abbot the Rights of Advowson of the Church of St. Helen Parish Church of Garstang Church-Town. The Parish was registered as being in the Decanatus de Aymunderne in the Archdiaconate de Richemund. The Grant was confirmed in AD 1241 by John le Romaine Archdeacon of Richmond; fortified by Assent of Archbishop Walter Gray and the Dean and Chapter of York. It was finally sealed by a Bull of Pope Gregory IX in the fifteenth year of his Pontificate. The date of origin of this ancient church cannot be ascertained but it was well established in the early part of the 12th century. Dignified bearer of the proud title of Cathedral of the Fylde, St Helen's Church attracted all devout Christians to worship from a very wide area. In AD 1427 in response to an appeal from the inhabitants of Garstang the Archdeacon of Richmond granted them a Licence to hold Divine Service each week for a period of one year in the Chapel of Trinity which was situated at the rear of Carrick House and Market House. The large building opposite the Town Hall was the residence of Mr Richard Horrabin who provided a site for a new chapel in the large garden behind his home.

St. Helen's Church

Market Place Garstang

The Rev. M
Priest of
A
Born Feb
Ordained
Died Au

St. Mary

Opened Aug 15th 1858 by the Rt. F
Consecrated June 19th 1968 by th

The new chapel was completed in AD 1788 and was originally designed for a congregation of 500 but was enlarged later to accommodate a further 60. The building which still stands on its original site is now used as a Magistrates Court. In AD 1816 a small school was built in Back Lane near the Chapel and this also had to cope with ever-increasing numbers of pupils until a new larger school could be built. Indeed the twin problems of lack of accommodation in Church and School were becoming ever more pressing each year particularly during the summer months when large contingents of men came over from Ireland for the haytime and potato harvest. With the opening of the new cotton mills in Calder Vale and the consequent influx of workpeople and their families from the large manufacturing towns the situation became desperate and Father Hickey redoubled his efforts to obtain a site for a new church and school. In 1856 his prayers were answered and he was enabled to buy sufficient land in Bonds to accommodate a new church and school and to provide space for a much-needed cemetery.

The original Chapel in Back Lane

Calder Vale circa 1880

PARISH

Rev. J. Shuttleworth
Rev. John Barrow
Rev. W. Barnes
Rev. J. Rickaby
Rev. F. Worswick
Rev. R. Sumner
Rev. Arthur Story

CATHOLICK SCHOOL 1816

Original sign Plaq
in slate from the ol
School in Back La
Garstang

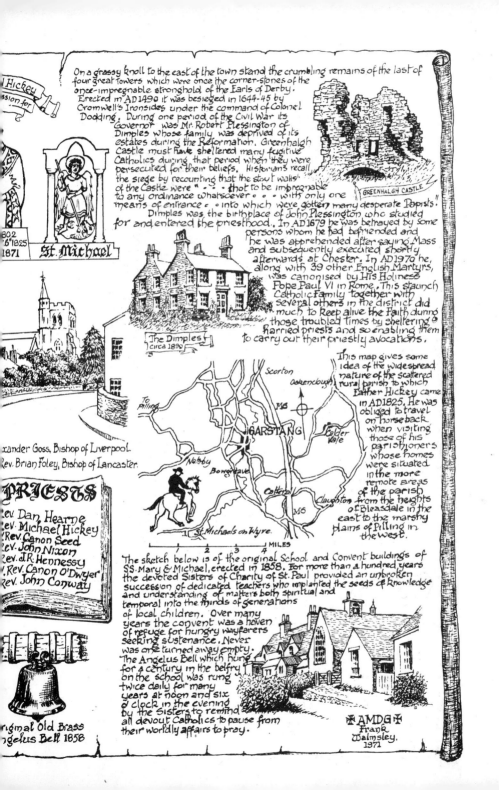

On a grassy knoll to the east of the town stand the crumbling remains of the last of four great towers which were once the corner-stones of the once-impregnable stronghold of the Earls of Derby. Erected in AD 1490 it was besieged in 1644-45 by Cromwell's Ironsides under the command of Colonel Dodding. During one period of the Civil War its Governor was Mr. Robert Plessington of Dimples whose family was deprived of its estates during the Reformation. Greenhalgh Castle must have sheltered many fugitive Catholics during that period when they were persecuted for their beliefs. Historians recall the siege by recounting that the stout walls of the Castle were " - - - that to be impregnable to any ordinance whatsoever o o o with only one means of entrance o o into which were gotten many desperate Papists." Dimples was the birthplace of John Plessington who studied for and entered the priesthood. In AD 1679 he was betrayed by some persons whom he had befriended and he was apprehended after saying Mass and subsequently executed shortly afterwards at Chester. In AD 1970 he, along with 39 other English Martyrs, was canonised by His Holiness Pope Paul VI in Rome. This staunch Catholic family together with several others in the district did much to keep alive the Faith during those troubled times by sheltering harried priests and so enabling them to carry out their priestly avocations.

GREENHALGH CASTLE

The Dimples circa 1890

St. Michael

802
16" 1825
1871

This map gives some idea of the widespread nature of the scattered rural parish to which Father Hickey came in AD 1825. He was obliged to travel on horseback when visiting those of his parishioners whose homes were situated in the more remote areas of the parish from the heights of Bleasdale in the east to the marshy plains of Pilling in the west.

Scorton
Oakenclough
M6
TO Pilling
GARSTANG
Calder Vale
Nateby
Bonds Gate
Catterall
M6
Claughton
St. Michael's on Wyre.
1 2 3 4 MILES

Hickey ssion for

xander Goss, Bishop of Liverpool.
Rev. Brian Foley, Bishop of Lancaster.

PRIESTS

ev. Dan Hearne
ev. Michael Hickey
Rev. Canon Seed
ev. John Nixon
ev. J.R. Hennessy
Rev. Canon O'Dwyer
ev. John Conway

The sketch below is of the original School and Convent buildings of SS. Mary & Michael, erected in 1858. For more than a hundred years the devoted Sisters of Charity of St. Paul provided an unbroken succession of dedicated teachers who implanted the seeds of knowledge and understanding of matters both spiritual and temporal into the minds of generations of local children. Over many years the convent was a haven of refuge for hungry wayfarers seeking sustenance. Never was one turned away empty. The Angelus Bell which hung for a century in the belfry on the school was rung twice daily for many years at noon and six o'clock in the evening by the Sisters to remind all devout Catholics to pause from their worldly affairs to pray.

riginal Old Brass
ngelus Bell 1858

✠ AMDG ✠
Frank
Walmsley.
1971

In 1864 a new railroad was laid between Garstang town and Pilling and the new train service put into operation on December 5th 1870. All sorts of troubles beset the line and such was the drain of funds that the service was discontinued until 1878. Not until 1908 was this local line extended to the long-planned terminus of Knott-End-on-Sea, thus becoming officially the Garstang and Knott End Railway. In 1923 it was absorbed by the London, Midland and Scottish Railway Company, but by 1930 all passenger traffic had been discontinued. The little engines of the line will long be remembered as characters in their own right. *Hebe*, the solitary, worked sixteen hours a day non-stop. The *Farmer's Friend*, hired during 1875, became known as *The Pilling Pig* because of its plaintive whistle and this nickname eventually adhered to the whole line. The photograph above shows the engine *Knott End* taking on water.

Right: The Preston to Kendal Canal, under construction for several years, was put into operation in November 1797, its purpose being to transport coal to North Lancashire and Westmorland and bring back limestone. Two wharves were constructed as near to the centre of Garstang as possible. The photograph shows part of the Aldcliffe stretch in 1910.

The right to hold a market on Thursday each week at Garstang and in addition a fair of two days' duration on the vigil and Day of the Feast of Saint Peter and Saint Paul (June 28th and 29th) was granted in the fourth year of Edward the Second's reign to the abbots of Cockersand. Dissolution of the Abbey probably caused the privilege to lapse for a time but on January 13th 1597 Queen Elizabeth the First granted "to the inhabitants of the Towne of Garstange for the relief of the poore of the same Towne, a weekly market to be kept upon the streetwaie and also Two Faires yearly". The second fair granted by Elizabeth was held upon St. Martin's Day in winter. This charter established the separate identities of Garstang Churchtown and Garstang Market Town.

"Garstang hath a great market for corn, cattle, yarn and fish," quoted Blome, the map maker. It was also well known for cheese. The steps of the Market Cross were used for laying out wares. Spirited bargaining over some prices ensued, but the price of eggs was fixed. Old-established businesses like Cartmell's and Storey's could always be relied upon. The delivery cart is pictured near Mr Holmes, the postman, outside Storey's Grocers and Confectioners.

Above: The Over-Wyre community for hundreds of years had to be sturdily independent and self-supporting because of its isolation. Names and occupations taken at random from old directories show this: mole catcher; joiner; wheelwright; oatcake baker; saddler; potato, hay and straw dealer; blacksmith; cooper; nail maker. The farm names speak history: Green Dick's; Union; Fold House; Smallwood Hey; Moss Side; Throstle Nest. Like Arnside Knot and Hard Knot, Knot End consisted of heaps of stones (Great and Little Knot), boulder stones of Scandinavian origin, but these were mutilated in harbour improvements for the Port of Fleetwood. The railway station at Knot End "on one of the most interesting and unique railways in the United Kingdom" has disappeared. In 1875 only three trains did the trip every day and an item on the time table read: "the evening train from Pilling to Garstang will proceed to the junction provided the extra fares amount to 3/-". The Garstang Engine Company leased the *Hope* to the Railway in 1883, eventually replaced by *Jubilee Queen* and *New Century*.

Right: The Bourne Arms Hotel adjoining the Railway Station and the Ferry Slip advertised a splendid Bowling Green and a New Grill Room in the Knot End and Garstang Penny Guide. Mr A. Gilbert was then proprietor and the ice cream was famous. Police constable, railway porter and yokel waiting for "opening time" belong to the leisurely days of that unique railway. This fine photograph was taken by H. H. Nickson in June 1901.

A grand procession took place on Tuesday October 25th 1887, when a large crowd assembled in Market Place at 2.45 and was led by the Garstang Flute and Drum Band to the site of the new Liberal Club. After the ceremony all marched back to the Royal Oak Hotel where a public luncheon was held. With speeches and musical items celebration went on until 7 o'clock. The upstairs of this club, known as the Assembly Rooms, was to prove a boon to all local people regardless of political bias. A large ballroom occupying the full width of the building was the scene of many a dance, play and concert. The local branch of the United Order of Catholic Brethren held their annual New Year Dance here and the children from Bonds performed their annual school concert on the stage. "Threepenny Hops", informal dances, where the men paid 3d admission fee but the ladies were admitted free of charge, were very popular. A group of local young ladies known as *The Mountebanks* put on fund-raising concerts during 1914–18. Two amateur dramatic societies staged plays in the winter. Eventually the whole property was sold to the County Council who converted the large room into a Magistrates' Courthouse.

Above and right: The fancy dress parade features "Votes for Women", and the Whitsuntide scene of about 1910 shows off the little girls' finery.

Nateby Agricultural Show. Right: Mr T. H. Watson (holding a stick) and his wife standing second from left, are with Mr and Mrs Shorrocks (on the right). Mr Watson owned farms in the Garstang area which were managed by Mr Shorrocks. Not far away is Bowers House, a small manor house which contained a priest-hole approached by winding stairs. Late Georgian windows and a front door have been inserted into a much earlier house and it is now a restaurant. Between Bowers House and Nateby Hall, it is supposed, there was once a secret passage.

Dairywomen who, in proportion to the number of cows they had, made the greatest quantity of cheese within the year, could win £3 at the shows. The tenant who grew the best crops of beans in drills won a silver cup. Finlayson's Patent Harrow, "sagaciously constructed . . . and so simple in principle that the dullest farm labourer could use it . . ." was obtained from Caton's, ironmongers, Preston. A man who infringed the patent was fined £50.

An advertisement in 1867 in a London journal revealed that the "Lordship of Garstang" was to be sold by auction, "comprising almost the whole of the important Market Town of Garstang". The manor had been inherited by the Reverend W. A. Walpole-Keppel, a Norfolk Rector who was unlikely to visit his Lancashire estates. The Bill of Sale makes interesting reading and mentions shops, private dwelling houses, hotels and inns, a dissenting chapel, a rope manufactory, farms, agricultural buildings, "capital waterside premises", a malt house, a lime kiln, coal and timber yard, three blacksmiths' shops and a bowling green. Very few of the properties, however, were sold and another descendant tried again in 1919 on November 27th and 28th. The printed schedule of this sale is again a mine of information about the life of the town, habits and inhabitants, rights of way, rentals and other charges.

A number of houses in Bridge Street are mentioned: Mr W. Lang, Plumber and Painter (rent £15-10-0 per annum), the County Constabulary (Lot 2), John Ball's Cottage (rent £4-14-0 per annum), Thomas Whiteside's and Arthur Breakell's (rentals £6-19-0 each).

Above and right: Two typical Garstang street scenes in 1900.

Top left: 1904, Ladies Hill, Pilling, pictures a white cottage, having clay walls re-inforced with straw, wattle and daub, the front door opening straight into the kitchen. Oak settle, stuffed birds under glass domes, antimacassars, heavy green "bobbled" chenille table-cloth, matching curtains and a solemn ticking clock would almost certainly have met the eye. In the nineteenth century small "coyts" were cleverly roofed with old boats in the short cut from Cartgate, Lindle Lane, leading to the old salt mines. Hundreds of years ago salt was extracted at the salt cotes by boiling sea-water over turf fires until only salt remained. This was also done at Stalmine and Lytham. In 1827 brass pans for this purpose were dug out of the peat at Foxhall. In a search for haematite ore in the 1870s a valuable bed of rock salt was discovered at Preesall, but not mined until 1889. The United Alkali Company was extracting at the rate of 4,000 tons a week by 1907 and the salt, so hard it had to be blasted, was known for its whiteness. It was sent to India, the Baltic, Canada, Faroes and Iceland. Trucks ran to Preesall jetty (bottom left), shown in 1936, where the salt was loaded onto steamers.

Above: Preesall Urban District Council's steamroller from 1910 is obviously the pride and joy of the village.

Above: Whitsun Fancy Dress Parade; Ted Hoyles sits on the shafts of his cart.

Right: The clock of the Town Hall can be seen in this photograph of Coronation Day, 1911. In 1750 the Town Hall was destroyed by a fire which burned all the historical documents. A new building appeared five years later, but in 1939 the Town Hall was again burned out. As on Whit Mondays, Coronation Day 1911 was celebrated by draping flags and bunting everywhere. White frocks and best suits were worn with shiny shoes, and the Calder Vale Band would arrive with newly-pressed uniforms and glittering musical instruments.

On May 27th 1974, the day of the Annual Whitsuntide Fair, just two months after the final meeting of Garstang Rural District Council, Mr Jonathan Greenhow became the first Mayor, following the new Local Government arrangements which brought such drastic changes all over the country. He was formally invested with his chain of office by Councillor Geoffrey J. Gornall, retiring Chairman of the Garstang Parish Council. The ceremony took place in the entrance hall of the Town Hall with two members of the newly-created Corporation bearing the halberds handed down from the old Corporation to the Town Trust. A procession round the town, led by the new Mayor, carried on the tradition of ceremony and procession, so long a feature of Garstang life.

41

The scattered gables of Garstang were seen by the poet and novelist William Black over a hundred years ago when there were 155 houses in the town. The entire population was then only 687 and even before the outbreak of World War I there were only 836 inhabitants. There are now more than 1,500 dwelling houses and the 43 shops which supplied requirements in 1873 have doubled their number.

Above: The old shopkeepers lived over or behind their premises which gave the High Street both character and vitality. The old cottages nestling on each side of the street have been demolished or had re-designed fronts. High Street follows a winding course, roughly parallel with the river. The ancient cobblestones have disappeared. They paved the street from wall to wall and can now be seen as only a meagre triangle where the Market Cross stands.

Right: The early Victorian property shown in the upper photograph from 1909 has lost its ivy-covered front and leafy surroundings, and where the omnibus station now stands there was a neat row of white-washed cottages running down Fletcher's Weind, each with its small cottage garden. The first building on Bridge Street was the village smithy, with weathered brick walls and thick bottle-glass windows, its small yard often crowded with farm horses waiting to be shod.

44

Left: Pilling village, with the boys standing outside the blacksmith's shop and the spired church in the background, is of ancient origin. The old burial ground was abandoned in 1717 and is now almost obliterated. Built into a barn wall at Pilling Old Hall nearby were fragments of tombstones taken from the ancient churchyard. A subsequent churchyard is now also full, the church being used only for funeral services. G. Holden, minister, mathematician and calculator of tides, has left a sundial there dated 1766 and inscribed "Thus eternity approaches". Stone axes and crude weapons have been turned up and the recent find of an amber bead points to possible Bronze Age connections. Boan Hill could be the site of an ancient settlement or battlefield. The small hills of gravel and sand (drumlins) left in this area are from the ice age – Eagland Hill, Cogie Hill sites of early settlements. Pilling was included in the Royal Forest of Wyresdale and subject to forest laws, so no one could keep a hunting dog.

Above: Pilling Windmill, six storeys high and put up in 21 days by Christopher Myers in 1808, is shown on the banks of the Broadfleet river. There were no sails on it in 1916, for since 1900 it was worked by steam. A farm labourer once agreed to be tied to the windmill sails for a gallon of beer, but managed only one revolution then begged to be released.

Above: Dolly's Cottage, Knott End, now gone, was built probably in the sixteenth century and thatched. It was once the home of "Old Doilee", a lady who lived to such a great age she appeared as an engraving in the *Monthly Illustrated*, together with an article, written in the days before photography, describing how spotless was her cottage.

Right: The Boat houses, Knott-End-on-Sea, were once homes, permanent or holiday, converted from fishing boats, and were situated by the shallow earth cliffs of Hackensall Brows.

47